AF087621

ANXIETY IS REALLY STRANGE.

'Like most anxiety sufferers, my anxiety doesn't manifest itself in rational ways. So I could be with a killer and not feel alarmed but then take my dogs for a walk and be debilitated with terror they'll run into the road' (Jon Ronson (2011), author of *The Psychopath Test*, on the strangeness of anxiety).

'Anxiety disorders are the most common type of psychiatric disorders in the US. lifetime prevalence of anxiety disorders among American adults is 28.8%' (B 2017). That's more than 1 in 4 people who are seriously affected by anxiety!

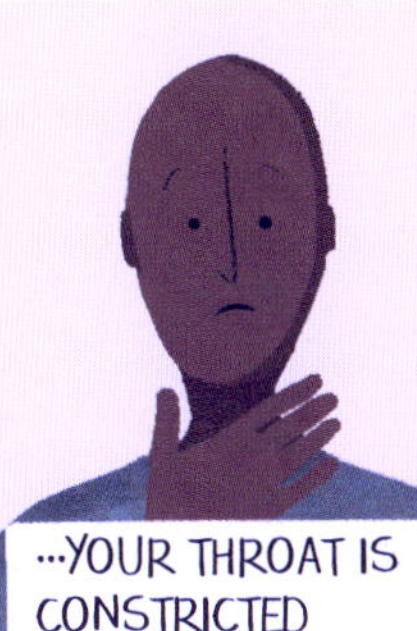

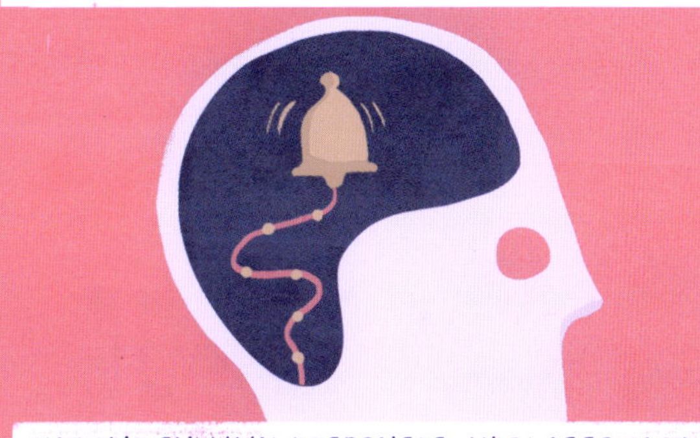

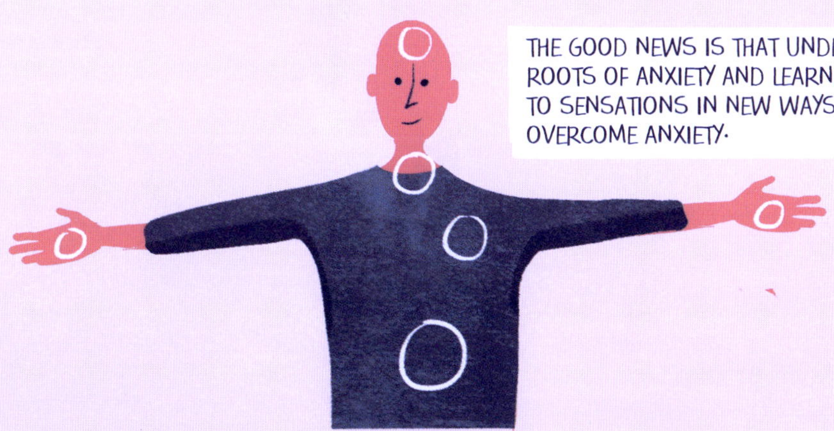

ople use "panic attack" very casually out here in LA, but I don't think most of m really know what it is. Every breath is laboured. You are dying. You are going die. It's terrifying. And then when the attack is over, the depression is still there' median Sarah Silverman 2015).

Anxiety 'is a natural reaction to perceived threat and is manifested cognitively (e.g. racing thoughts), physiologically (e.g. autonomic arousal), and behaviorally (e.g. escape).' People 'with anxiety disorders experience frequent false alarms that cause substantial distress and functional impairment' (Blakey & Abramowitz 2016).

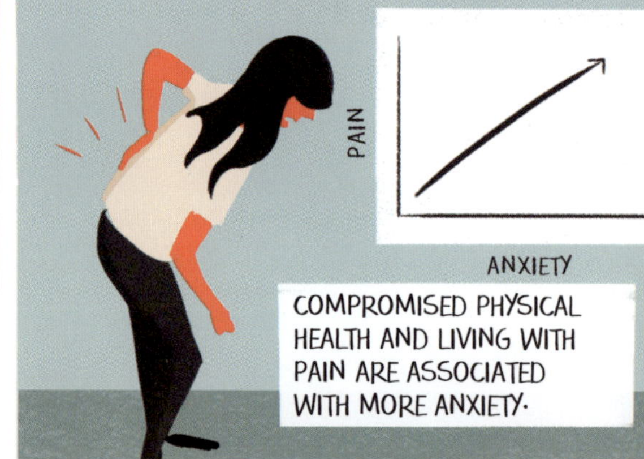

This section on causes of anxiety draws heavily on Mind's free leaflet on anxiety and panic attacks. I worked for Mind in London for 8 years. It is an excellent UK charity that offers consistently good, user-led advice and services for people with mental-health issues (www.mind.org.uk).

'Anxiety disorders appear to be caused by an interaction of biopsychosocial factors including genetic vulnerability, which interact with situations, stress, or trauma to produce clinically significant syndromes' (Bhatt 2017). Health always depends on the interplay of biology, psychology and society (Moseley & Butler 2017).

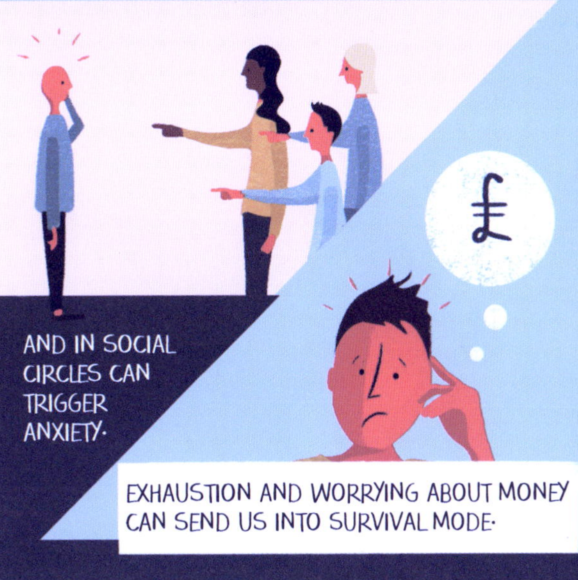

ADVERSE CHILDHOOD EXPERIENCES (ACES) ARE AN IMPORTANT CAUSE OF ANXIETY. THE 'ACE STUDY' IS A LANDMARK RESEARCH STUDY, STARTED IN 1998, WHICH ASSESSES THE IMPACT OF CHILDHOOD TRAUMA.

YOU CAN CHECK YOUR ACE SCORE FROM A LIST OF 10 EVENTS, SUCH AS PERSONAL ABUSE OR NEGLECT OR LIVING IN A FAMILY WITH ALCOHOLISM, MENTAL ILLNESS OR A DISAPPEARED PARENT.

THE HIGHER YOUR SCORE, THE GREATER RISK YOU HAVE OF POOR MENTAL AND PHYSICAL HEALTH.

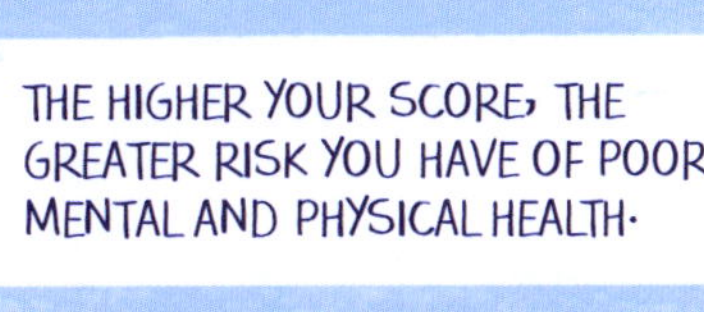

'There are 10 types of childhood trauma measured in the ACE Study... Each type of trauma counts as one. So a person who's been physically abused, with one alcoholic parent, and a mother who was beaten up has an ACE score of three' (from the wonderful www.acestoohigh.com).

'1 in 8 people have 4 or more ACEs... For a person with an ACE score of four or more their relative risk of chronic obstructive pulmonary disease was two and a half times that of someone with an ACE score of zero. ... For depression, it was four and a half times' (Dr Burke Harris 2015).

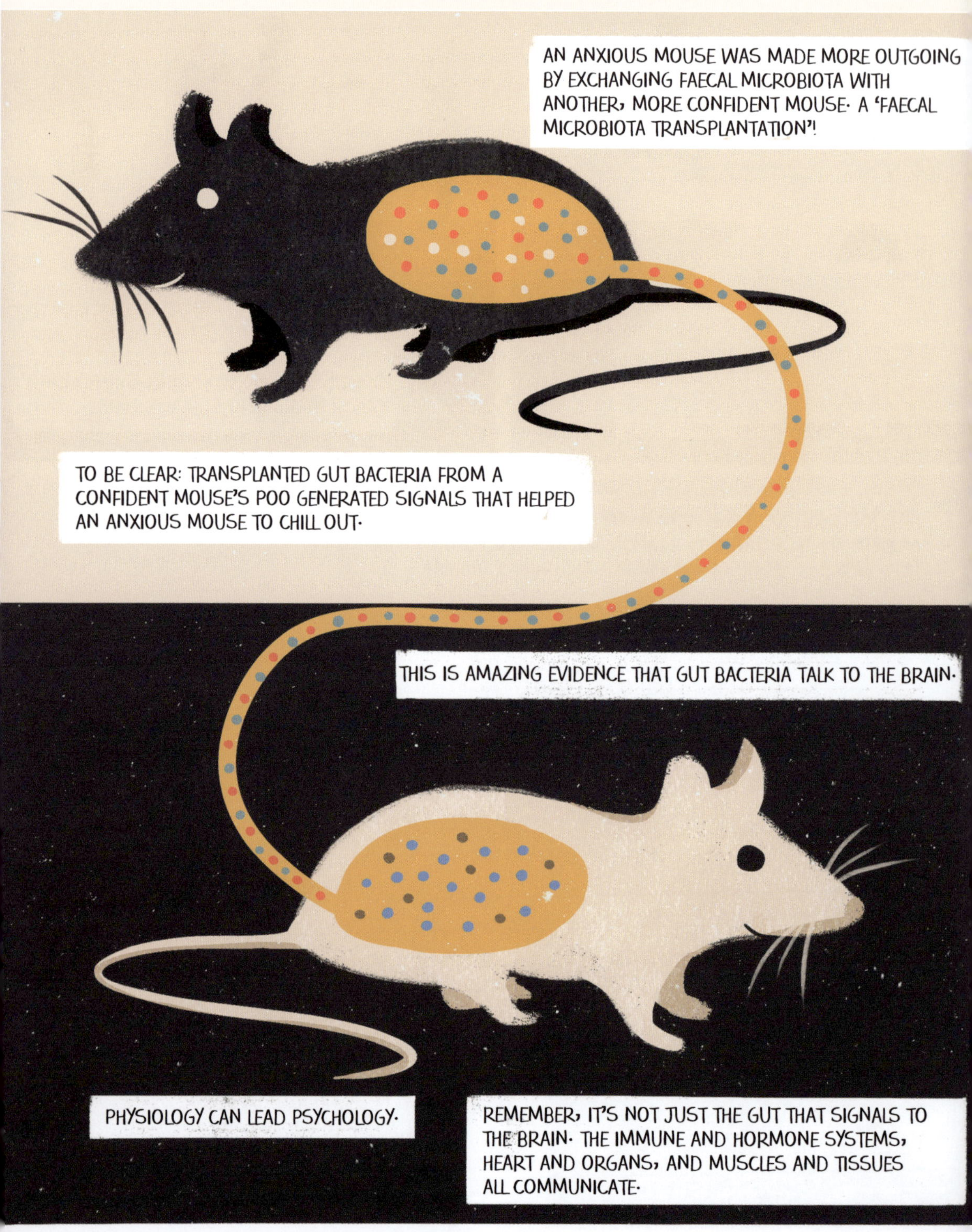

here is growing evidence in humans and in mice that 'the intestinal microbiome nfluences the brain and behavior', i.e. there is a 'gut microbiome-to-brain axis' Collins et al 2013). 'Gut-brain communication' links 'anxiety disorders and... nflammatory bowel disease' (Neufeld et al 2011; Temperton 2015).

'Some of the most devastating medical and public health problems of our time depression, substance addiction and intractable pain - are centred on pathologies feeling' (Damasio et al 2013). Good news: Craig (2015) states 'Your interocepti awareness is key to everything. It can be trained.'

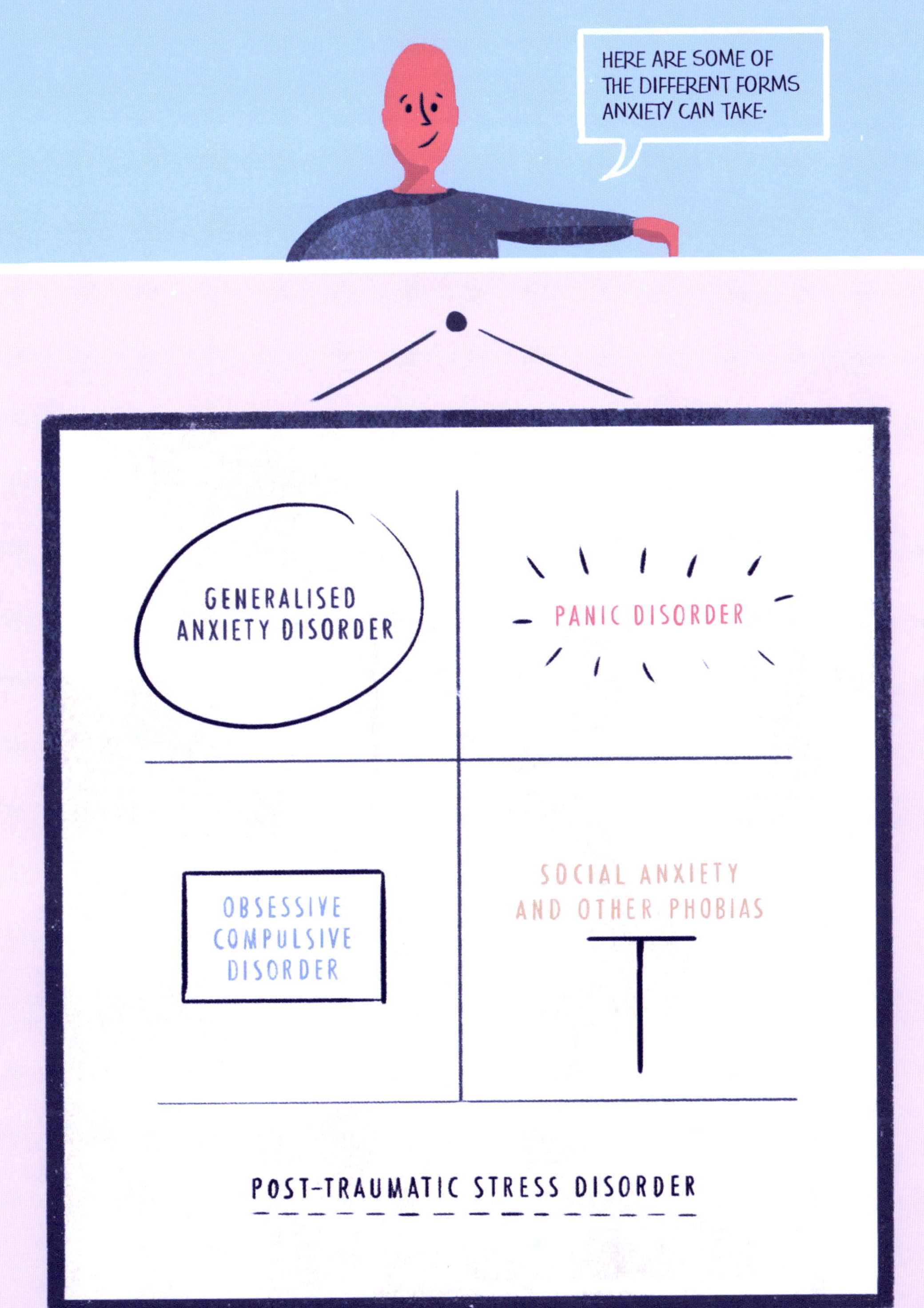

neralised anxiety disorder (GAD) includes a wide range of symptoms, but involves n-specific anxiety for extended periods. Your 'experience with GAD might be quite fferent from the problems another person experiences'. 'Panic disorder can mean at you feel constantly afraid of having another panic attack' (Mind 2017).

In OCD, 'unwelcome thoughts' that 'repeatedly appear in your mind' exist with 'repetitive activities that you feel you have to do'. 'If you have a phobia, your anxiety may be triggered by very specific situations or objects.' PTSD 'can feel like you're reliving al the fear and anxiety you experienced' during a trauma (Mind 2017).

Bakewell (2017), discussing Kierkegaard: 'constant choosing brings a pervasive anxiety, not unlike the vertigo that comes from looking over a cliff. It is not the fear of falling so much as the fear that you can't trust yourself not to throw yourself off.'

'The Second Sex was almost entirely occupied with the complex territory where free choice, biology and social and cultural factors meet and mingle to create a human being who gradually becomes set in her ways as life goes on' (Bakewell 2017 Simone de Beauvoir).

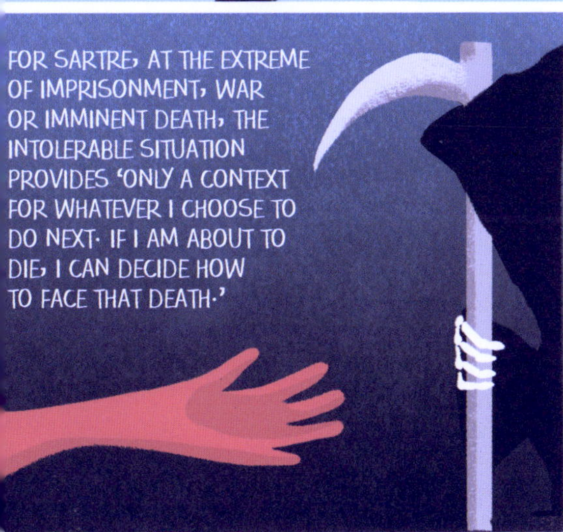

...hoices, influences and habits can accumulate over a lifetime to create a structure ...at becomes hard to break out of' (this, and other quotes above, from Bakewell ...017). We are free to the extent that oppressive power structures, economics and ...cietal norms allow.

'History, despite its wrenching pain, cannot be unlived, but if faced with courage, nee... not be lived again.' The incomparable Maya Angelou (1993) reminds us that courag... is needed to transcend our past.

IF SOMETHING AS SEEMINGLY FIXED AS GENDER CAN BE SHAPED AND FORMED, THEN WE CAN BE HOPEFUL THAT THE RESPONSE TO THE PHYSIOLOGY UNDERPINNING ANXIETY CAN ALSO BE SHAPED AND REFORMED.

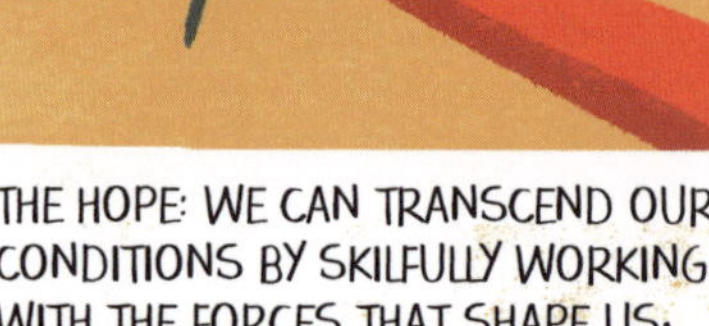

WE WILL LEARN THAT CURRENT NEUROSCIENCE, SPECIFICALLY THE MODEL OF CONSTRUCTED EMOTION, HELPS US EMBRACE A 'RADICAL FREEDOM' TO BE MORE THAN OUR BIOLOGY. WE CAN BE MORE THAN OUR ANXIETY.

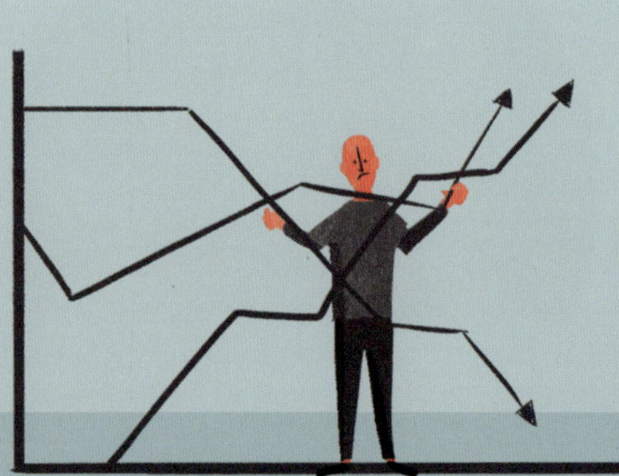

There is no doubt that our biology, a mix of chemistry, reflexes and behaviours, is the root of emotion. But it does not determine us. Physiological shifts are powerful factors to be considered in our emergent awareness. 'Hacking' our biology gives us more tools to shape our experience.

'Radical freedom' is a liberating Sartre phrase that is deeply hopeful when applied to individuals. The existentialists were also intensely concerned with politics and 'subtle mechanisms of oppression'; freedom is 'the topic underlying all others' and is both personal and political (Bakewell 2017).

THE CORE MODEL OFFERED HERE IS THAT ANXIETY ALWAYS INVOLVES GETTING STUCK IN PROTECTIVE DEFENSE CASCADES OF 'FIGHT-OR-FLIGHT' OR 'FREEZE'. THE PERCEPTION OF THREAT CAN BE TRIGGERED BY EVENTS INSIDE THE BODY, INSIDE THE MIND OR FROM THE ENVIRONMENT.

bert Saplosky (2017): 'you're not going to get anywhere if you think there's going be the brain region or the hormone or the gene or the childhood experience or the olutionary mechanism that explains everything. Instead, every bit of behavior has ultiple levels of causality.'

'The brain areas and neuromodulatory systems that contribute to fear and anxiety exhibit great overlap' (Tovote et al 2015). Kozlowska et al (2015) describe 'the defence cascade'; anxiety is associated with mobilisation (fight-or-flight) and immobilisation (freeze/dissociation); prior learning affects whether you fight or flee or freeze.

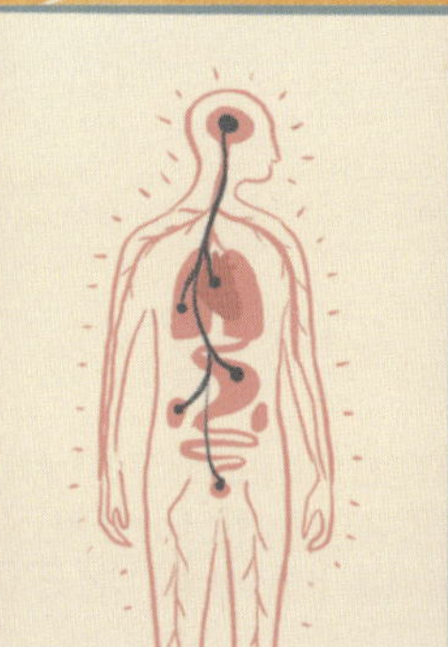

human being in perfection ought always to preserve a calm and peaceful mind, and ever allow passion or a transitory desire to disturb his tranquillity' (Mary Shelley 818). Her classic Victorian gothic novel *Frankenstein* can be seen as a complex xploration of the consequences of unbalanced rationality and excess emotion.

'Darwin argued that...emotional expressions are not just universal across cultures, but ha their roots in purposeful, and similar, animal behaviours across many mammilian specie Darwin's basic thesis helped 'usher forth the robust scientific study of emotional experien and 'has been elaborated, refined, studied and debated ever since' (Zolli 2015).

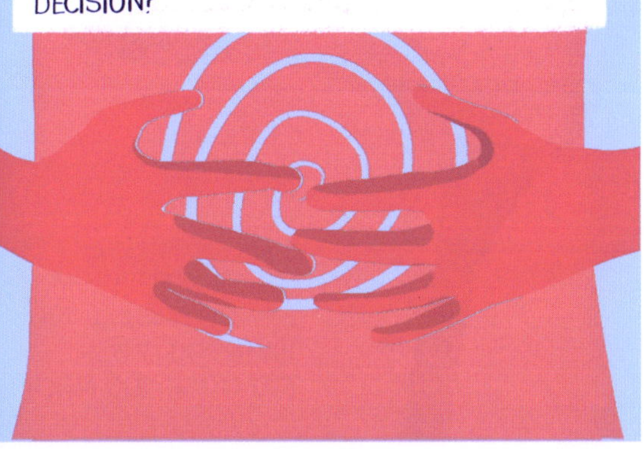

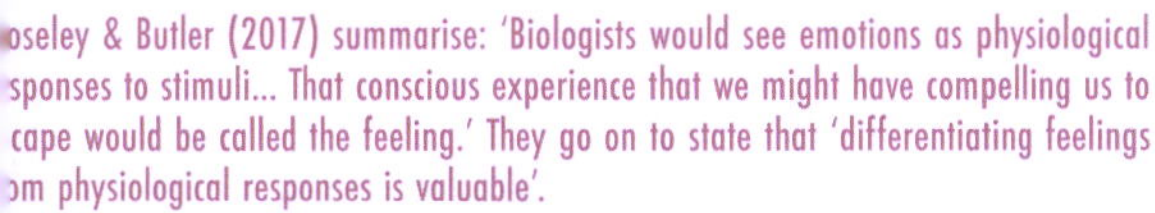

Moseley & Butler (2017) summarise: 'Biologists would see emotions as physiological responses to stimuli… That conscious experience that we might have compelling us to escape would be called the feeling.' They go on to state that 'differentiating feelings from physiological responses is valuable'.

Scientists use a confusing mix and match of terms. For body phenomena: 'physiology', 'behaviour', 'reflexes', 'affect' (Barrett 2017), 'drives', 'emotions' (Damasio et al 2013). For awareness of body phenomena: 'emotions' (Barrett 2017), 'feelings' (Damasio et al 2013), 'homeostatic emotions' (Craig 2015).

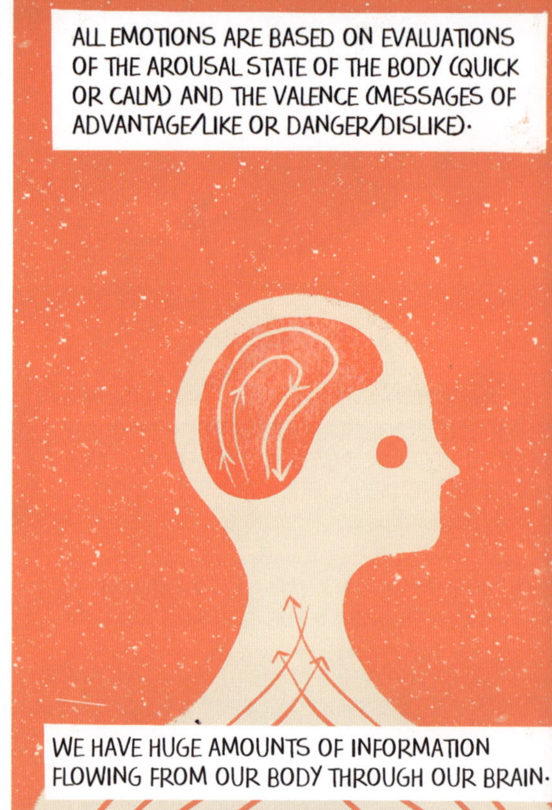

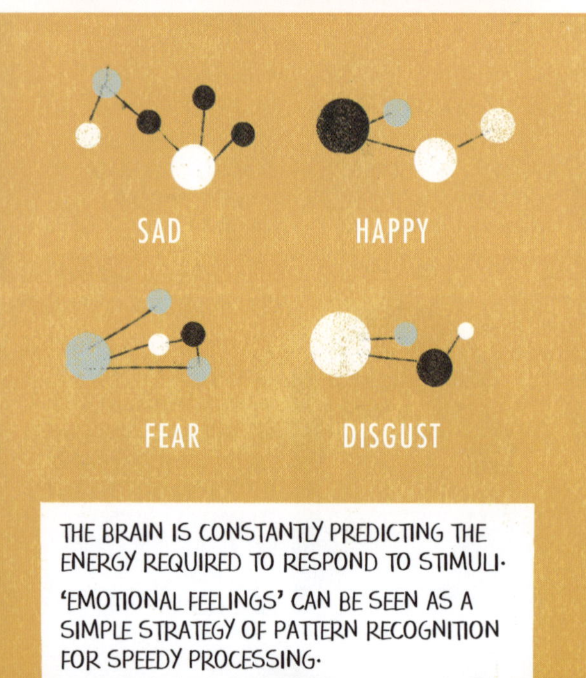

The efficient use of energy is what biology is organised to perform.' 'It is essential to recognise that homeostasis drives behaviour.' 'All of our behaviour is emotional.' Interoception is 'sensory input representing the condition of the entire body' (Craig 2015).

'A feeling is an interoceptive construct that the brain uses to represent the over energy costs and benefits of any actual or potential emotional behavior, that homeostatic valuation' (Craig 2015). 'Emotional states are automatic signals danger and advantage' (Damasio and Le Doux 2013).

HIGHLY INFLUENTIAL WORK BY PAUL ECKMAN OFFERED THAT EMOTIONS ARE ESSENTIALLY THE SAME FOR ALL HUMAN BEINGS.

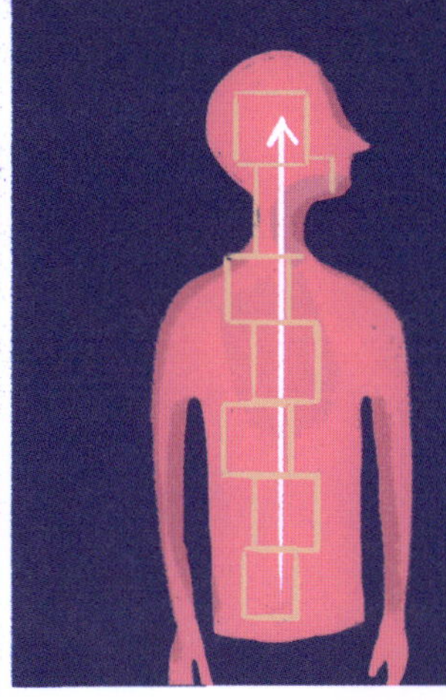

HARD-WIRED CIRCUITS INSIDE THE BRAIN ARE SAID TO COMPETE TO GENERATE DISTINCT EMOTIONS SUCH AS FEAR, DISGUST, ANGER, JOY, SADNESS.

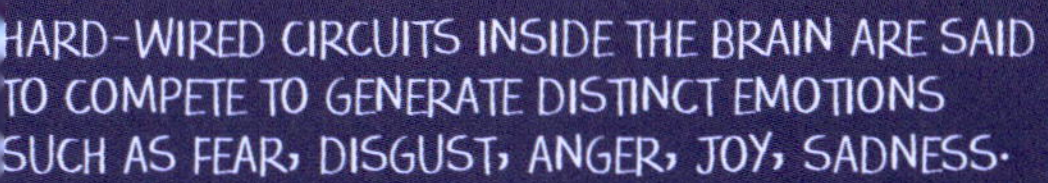

THE CHALLENGE TO THE HARD-WIRED MODEL IS THE SHEER VARIETY OF WAYS THAT WE CAN EXPRESS EMOTIONS.

WE CAN CLENCH OUR FISTS IN HAPPINESS AS OUR TEAM WINS. WE CAN DISSOLVE IN HAPPINESS AT THE CARESS OF A LOVER. WE CAN EVEN CRY WITH HAPPINESS.

A QUICK DETOUR TO SHOW ANXIETY IS NOT ALL BAD.

kman showed pictures of actors' faces to hunter-gatherers in Papua New Guinea. He aimed they were able to name the distinct, universal emotions shaped by evolution. e 'Facial Action Coding System' analyses face muscles to create 'the first objective easure of specific emotion' (Keltner 2009).

The variability in expression 'suggests that emotions are as much cultural signals a they are biological ones' (Zolli 2015). Barrett (2017) critiques Ekman; attempts t replicate his research in Namibia did not work, she is damning on using actors' face and the priming of subjects in the original studies.

'ANXIETY IS A GOOD THING BECAUSE PSYCHOPATHS DON'T HAVE ANY.' JON RONSON
ANXIETY IS A NORMAL FEATURE OF BEING HUMAN, WITHOUT IT WE CAN BECOME COLD AND CALCULATING. JON RONSON'S AMAZING QUOTE SUGGESTS THAT A LACK OF ANXIETY IS A TRAIT OF PSYCHOPATHY!

ANXIETY CAN BE GOOD· IT HELPS US PREPARE AND NOT BE OVERCONFIDENT·
INFLUENTIAL RESEARCH FROM 1908 SHOWED THAT A LITTLE BIT OF ANXIETY AND AROUSAL HELPS US PERFORM BETTER· TRY REFRAMING 'I AM ANXIOUS' TO 'THERE IS A PROTECTIVE FEELING OF GETTING READY FOR ACTION'· NOT QUITE AS SNAPPY, BUT MUCH MORE USEFUL·

CONCEPTS HELP US DECIDE WHETHER SOMETHING IS CAKE OR BREAD.

CAKE IS MADE FROM CLASSIC INGREDIENTS OF SUGAR, FLOUR, EGGS AND BUTTER.

WE CAN MAKE A POLENTA CAKE WITH CORN, MAPLE SYRUP AND COCONUT OIL - NONE OF THE CLASSIC INGREDIENTS BUT STILL, WE AGREE, IT FITS THE CONCEPT OF CAKE.

BRIOCHE IS ALSO MADE FROM SUGAR, FLOUR, EGGS AND BUTTER. DELICIOUS. BUT, WE AGREE, IT'S A TYPE OF BREAD.

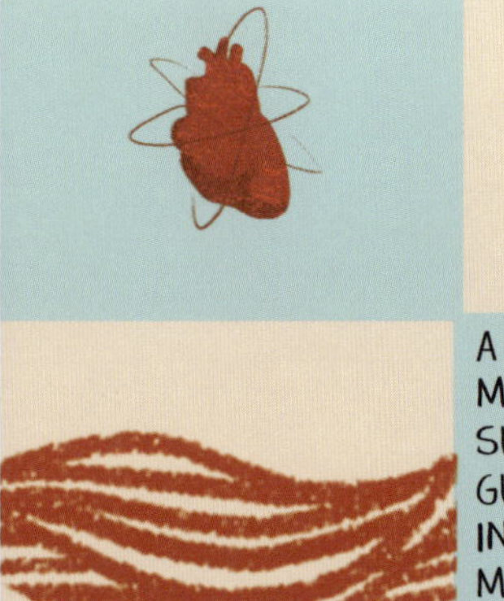

A QUICK HEART, BRACED MUSCLES, AN ADRENALINE SURGE, CHURNING GUTS ARE ALL-PURPOSE INGREDIENTS USED IN MANY EMOTIONS.

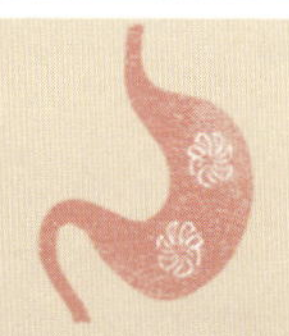

FEAR AND EXCITEMENT USE SIMILAR INGREDIENTS, JUST LIKE BREAD AND CAKE, BUT THE EXPERIENCE IS VERY DIFFERENT ACCORDING TO THE CONCEPT WE APPLY.

For simple tasks, increasing arousal continues to help us to be more focused, but, after helping initially, unchecked arousal 'impairs performance under more complex or challenging learning situations' (Diamond et al 2007 commenting on the influential Yerkes-Dobson graph from 1908).

'Emotions are not built-in but made from more basic parts. They are not universal vary from culture to culture. They are not triggered; you create them. They emerge a combination of the physical properties of your body, a flexible brain that wires itse whatever environment (culture and upbringing) it develops in' (Barrett 2017).

DID YOU KNOW THERE ARE EMOTIONS YOU HAVE NOT EXPERIENCED YET? TO FULLY KNOW AN EMOTION TAKES PRACTICE, UNDERSTANDING AND COMMUNITY. CULTURE TURNS A CONFUSED MORASS OF FEELINGS INTO A FORM WE CAN INHABIT.

GERMAN
SCHADENFREUDE

IN ENGLISH THERE IS NO EQUIVALENT WORD TO THE GERMAN 'SCHADENFREUDE'. THE PACKAGE 'JOY AT ANOTHER'S DISCOMFORT' IS NOVEL FOR ENGLISH SPEAKERS.

DANISH
HYGGE

'HYGGE' IS A DANISH WORD THAT SUMMARISES A STATE OF COSINESS, EASE AND COMFORT THAT DANES INSTANTLY GET, BUT NON-DANES HAVE TO WORK OUT.

HEBREW
FIRGUN

'FIRGUN' IS 'DELIGHT IN ANOTHER'S SUCCESS' IN HEBREW.

FILIPINO
LIGET

'LIGET' IS AN EMOTION THAT ANTHROPOLOGIST RENATO ROSALDO STRUGGLED TO GRASP WHILE LIVING WITH AN ISOLATED FILIPINO TRIBE IN THE 1960S. IT WAS USED FOR ENERGETIC 'BOUNDING UP A TRAIL', 'COLLECTIVE GRIEF' AND 'UNMOORED' CHAOTIC VIOLENCE.

YEARS LATER, THE MEANING SHIFTED FOR ROSALDO, FROM A 'STERILE' UNDERSTANDING TO A LIVED EXPERIENCE. IN THE INTENSITY OF HOWLING OVER THE DEATH OF HIS WIFE, HE DISCOVERED LIGET AS 'HIGH-VOLTAGE' ALIVENESS.

ur brain makes emotion as it needs it, on the spot, using a set of all-purpose redients. So the same brain networks that make emotion also make thoughts, and mories and perceptions' (Barrett 2017). 'Liget' quotes are from an interview with nato Rosaldo, Invisibilia on NPR (Spiegel 2017).

'Perception...has to be a process of informed guesswork in which the brain combines sensory signals with its prior expectations or beliefs about the way the world is to form its best guess of what caused those signals.' 'We don't just passively perceive the world, we actively generate it' (Seth 2017).

THE CONSTRUCTED EMOTION MODEL STATES THAT EMOTIONS ARE NOT HARD-WIRED.

THEY ARE NOT PART OF AN UNSTABLE HIERARCHY SANDWICHED BETWEEN BODY AND COGNITION.

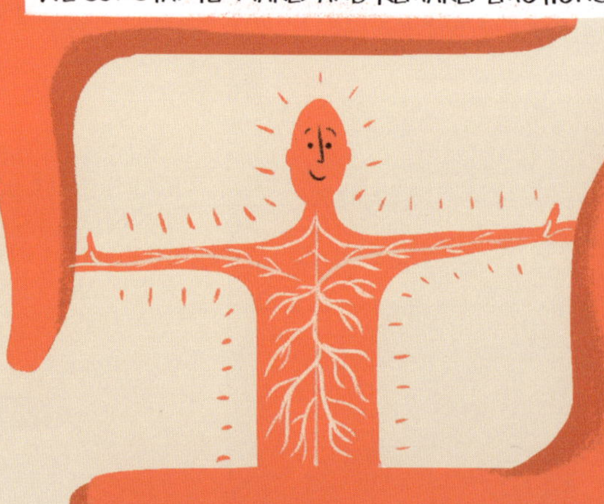

WE CONSTANTLY MAKE, AND REMAKE, EMOTIONS.

THINKING
PHYSIOLOGY
EMOTIONS
MEMORY
CONSCIOUSNESS
PERCEPTION

EMOTIONS ALWAYS CO-EMERGE WITH MEMORY AND THINKING. FEELINGS ARE ALWAYS PART OF PERCEPTION AND ARE FUNDAMENTAL TO CONSCIOUSNESS.

WE DO NOT HAVE TO BECOME VICTIMS OF FLAWED 'EMOTION CIRCUITS'. THERE AREN'T ANY. WE CAN REFRAME OUR EXPERIENCE.

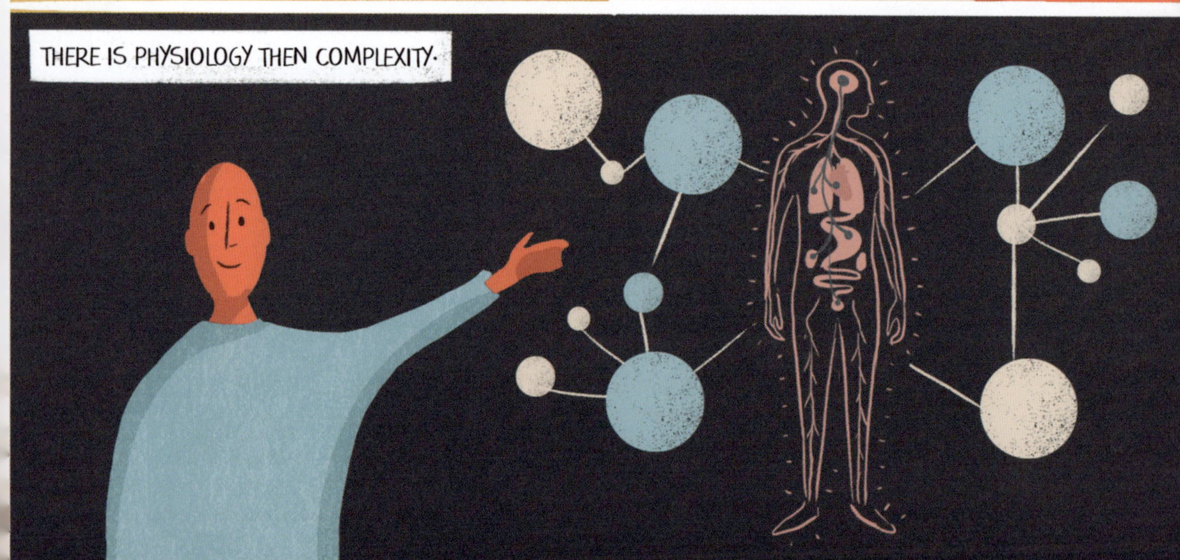

THERE IS PHYSIOLOGY THEN COMPLEXITY.

BRAINS PREDICT AND PROTECT.
WE ARE QUICK TO PREDICT DISASTER, USING OUR WORST MEMORIES AS A TEMPLATE.

IN ANXIETY WE ARE ALWAYS READY WITH THE FINGER ON THE BIG RED BUTTON. THE BUTTON THAT SHOULD BE PRESERVED FOR LIFE-OR-DEATH SITUATIONS.

THIS IS THE PROBLEM OF ANXIETY DISORDERS (AND PERSISTENT PAIN, TIREDNESS, CHRONIC INFLAMMATION AND DISSOCIATION).

WITH SKILL, UNDERSTANDING AND PRACTICE WE CAN CATCH THE ALARM SYSTEMS IN ACTION. WE CAN NEGOTIATE, ORIENT TO WHAT IS ACTUALLY HAPPENING AND ACT OUT A NEW POSSIBILITY.

REMEMBER, HOWEVER, THE DANGER SENSORS GO DEEP. WE NEED TO MANAGE THE COMPLEX INTERPLAY OF PHYSIOLOGICAL REFLEXES, FAMILY TRIGGERS AND OPPRESSIVE CULTURE.

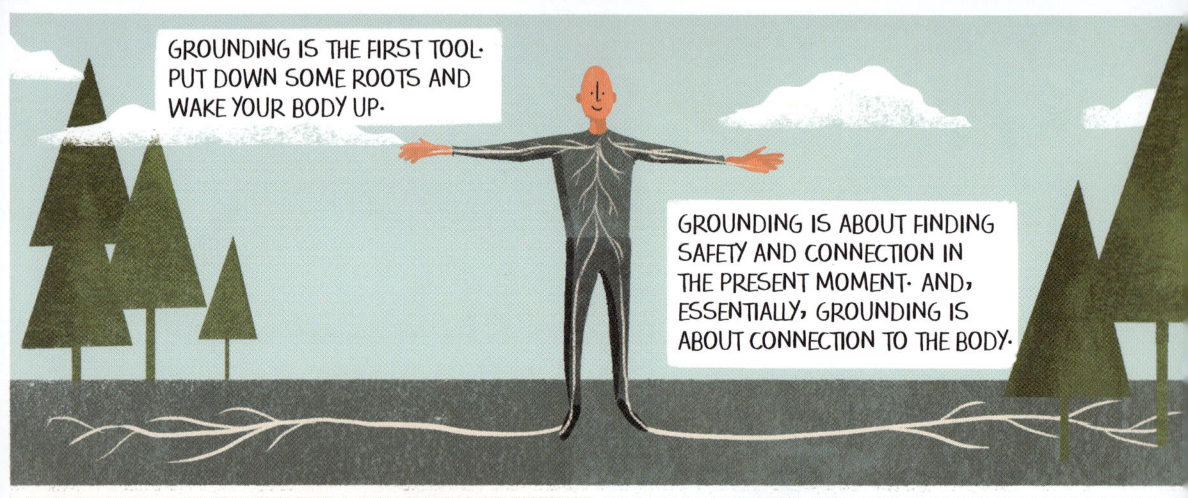

'To manage the pain of early trauma, some individuals disconnect from their bodies and live in their minds. They value thinking and logic over feelings and emotions. Other individuals, having never embodied, manage their disconnection by spiritualising their experience…

These individuals tend to live in the energetic field, in more ethereal realms.' Peo who are not connected to their bodies 'when asked what are they feeling in their be find the question challenging, anxiety provoking, and often impossible to answ (Heller & LaPierre 2012).

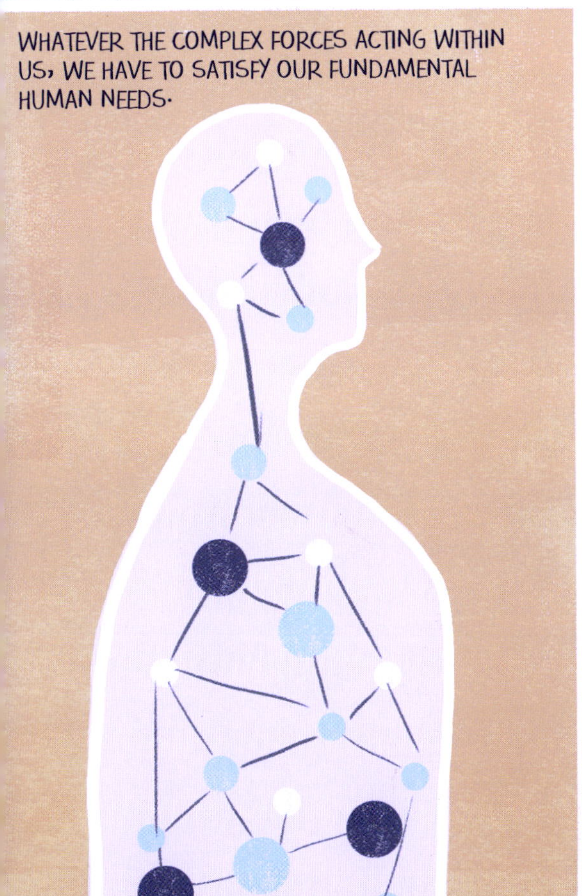

'Doing the right thing" is always context dependent.' 'We are always being shaped / seemingly irrelevant stimuli, subliminal information, and internal forces we don't now a thing about' (Sapolsky 2017). For HALT in addiction see Powers (2016).

A 'startling' study showed that judges, paragons of rationality, are meaner if they are hungry or tired. In 2011 researchers reviewed 1100 judicial rulings and found judges were far more likely to grant prisoners parole just after they had eaten or at the start of the day (Sapolsky 2017).

Awe is 'being in the presence of something vast, beyond current understanding'. William James recommended awe to create a ''blissful equanimity' free from anxieties' (Bergland 2017). Distraction can help anxiety: 'When your thinking brain — the prefrontal cortex — is highly engaged, it slams the brakes on feelings' (Barker 2017).

'Most positive emotions are arousing and engage the "fight-or-flight" response'; 'notably awe has the opposite effect'. Awe optimises the control of the heart by increasing the activity in the vagus nerve. Research links awe to play, curiosity, imagination, and creativity; activities we can all do, even if not outside (Bergland 2017).

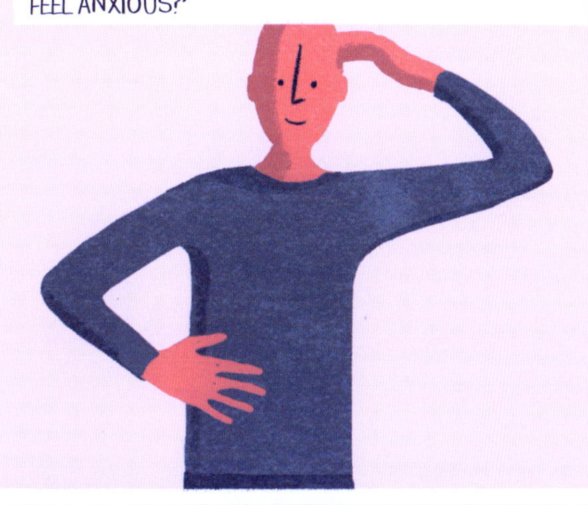

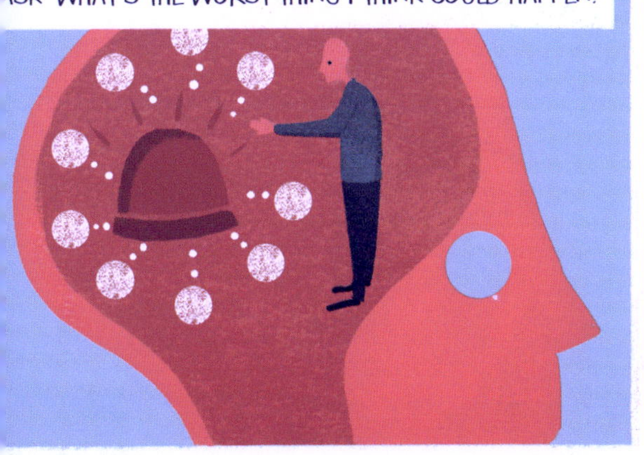

st because you feel it doesn't make it real. Feelings aren't a satellite dish receiving gnals of eternal truth.' 'Change the story and your feelings change' (Barker 2017). collapse, 'the most potent strategy is to move towards the fear, to contact the mobility itself and to consciously explore the various sensations' (Levine 2010).

'When the body becomes more physiologically regulated', this 'promotes opportunitie to feel safe and to develop trusting relationships.' 'Our thoughts can be bolder, more expansive and creative and perhaps even spiritual. These emergent features are no going to be expressed, if we're in the state of constant threat' (Porges 2016).

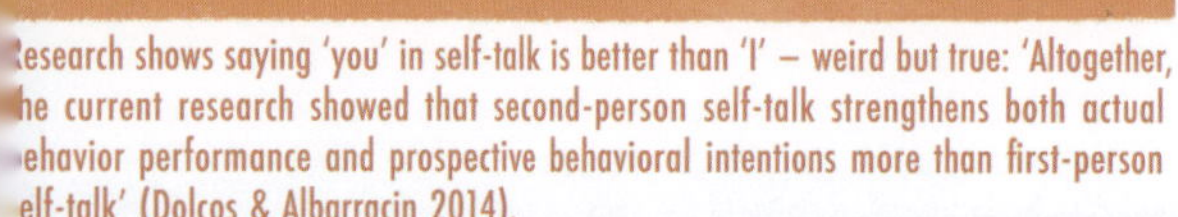
Research shows saying 'you' in self-talk is better than 'I' – weird but true: 'Altogether, the current research showed that second-person self-talk strengthens both actual behavior performance and prospective behavioral intentions more than first-person self-talk' (Dolcos & Albarracin 2014).

Anne Hathaway, filming *Les Misérables*: 'I closed my eyes and I remember thinking "Hathaway, if you do not do this in this moment, you have no right to call yourself an actor. ...just do your job." I opened my eyes and I'm like (snaps fingers): "Let's go." And I did it' (Dolcos & Albarracin 2014).

he storage and flow of information inside us changes as we respond to the world. ragments of memory that the brain suspects are dangerous can activate anxiety. The anger feels real but it's not happening right now. Health is the ability to manage ntense sensations in the present moment without being overwhelmed.

'Your in-breath will naturally lengthen when your out-breath is longer' (Boyes 201 and Herrero et al 2017). Levine (2010) recommends the sound 'Voo'; Alexande Technique (Soar 1999) uses 'The Whispered Ah'. Not 'Oh My God' but 'Orient Mov Ground'. OMG is explored more fully in *Trauma is Really Strange*.

'...raumatized people chronically feel unsafe inside their bodies: The past is alive in the ...rm of gnawing interior discomfort. Their bodies are constantly bombarded by visceral ...arning signs, and, in an attempt to control these processes, they often become expert ... ignoring their gut feelings and in numbing awareness' (van der Kolk 2015).

An early counter-intuitive approach is 'paradoxical intention' from Viktor Frankl (1946... 'The phobic patient is invited to intend, even if only for a moment, precisely that whic... he fears.' By this deliberate engagement 'the wind is taken out of the sails of anxiet... See also Wolitzky & Telch (2009) on 'oppositional actions' in exposure.

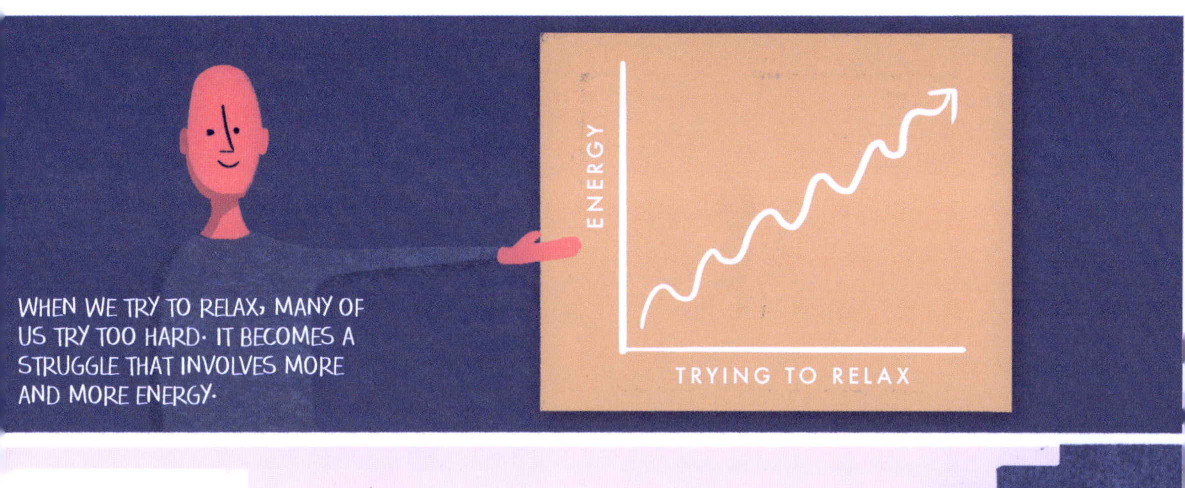

WHEN WE TRY TO RELAX, MANY OF US TRY TOO HARD. IT BECOMES A STRUGGLE THAT INVOLVES MORE AND MORE ENERGY.

A LOCKED SEAT BELT WILL SPRING OPEN, BUT ONLY IF YOU ALLOW IT TO CLOSE FOR A BIT.

SOMETIMES WE NEED TO GO BACKWARDS TO GO FORWARDS. TRY GOING INTO THE DIFFICULT FEELING.

GO SLOW, ALLOW FEELINGS ASSOCIATED WITH DISCHARGING TENSION; IT IS OK TO SHAKE A LITTLE BIT AND BREATHE DIFFERENTLY.

SELF-REGULATE BY PUTTING THE BRAKES ON ANYTHING TOO SPEEDY INSIDE YOU, OR HINTS OF BECOMING DREAMY.

BUT, DO NOT ALWAYS TRY TO RELAX, DO NOT GET STUCK PULLING ON A LOCKED SEAT BELT.

ce we can self-regulate the defence cascade, 'graded exposure' helps in working th anxiety. Pain and anxiety go hand in hand (Granot & Ferber 2005). Think of ilding resilience to anxiety as the same as exercising for strength. Graded exposure used to regulate pain and catastrophising (Moseley & Butler 2017).

'Exposure is considered the first-line intervention for anxiety disorders by internationa health care bodies.' 'The aim of exposure therapy from an inhibitory learning perspective is to help patients generate and strengthen inhibitory associations relative to older fearful associations' (Blakey & Abramowitz 2016).

MOST PEOPLE ASSUME FEELING IS EASY AND NATURAL: IT'S NOT. TO MOVE TOWARDS DIFFICULT FEELINGS AND THEN MOVE AWAY IS A HUGE SKILL.

FEEL A LITTLE BIT OF TENSION AND ANGST IN SHORT BURSTS. PRACTISE IN A CONTEXT WHERE YOU FEEL SAFE, MAYBE WITH A FRIEND.

IF NECESSARY, A BODY-ORIENTED THERAPIST CAN HELP YOU TO FEEL A LITTLE BIT, BUT NOT TOO MUCH.

1
2
3

WHEN STARTING OUT, TRY 30 SECONDS TO 2 MINUTES MAXIMUM FEELING THE DIFFICULT THING. GO REALLY SLOWLY. IN ANY ONE SESSION, EXPLORE FOR 3 SHORT TRIES ONLY, AND THEN REST AND TRY AGAIN ANOTHER DAY.

GOING INTO DIFFICULT FEELINGS CAN BE DONE AS A FORM OF GRADED EXPOSURE.

CHALLENGE AND RECOVER, CHALLENGE AND RECOVER. TAKE THE REST PHASES SERIOUSLY.

SOMETIMES YOU MAY FEEL WORSE; MAYBE DO LESS NEXT TIME...

...BUT BE PERSISTENT TO DEVELOP RESILIENCE.

THINK OF LEARNING NOT TO PANIC AS LIKE LEARNING TO MAKE LONG TREKS. YOU WILL NEED TO SLEEP WELL, EAT WELL AND PRACTISE. USE A GUIDE WHERE NEEDED AND TRY DIFFERENT ROUTES.

YOU START SLOWLY IN THE 'RECOVERY SPA' AND TAKE YOUR TIME IN THE 'SLOPES OF JUST FEELING SOMETHING'. MAKE SURE YOU AVOID FREEZING 'LAKE DISSOCIATION'.

YOU CAN PROGRESS TO THE 'FOOTHILLS OF SLIGHTLY SCARY AND QUICK'. PRETTY SOON YOU CAN MANAGE 'MOUNT REALLY QUITE ANXIOUS', VISITING THE 'VALLEY OF NAMELESS DREAD' ONLY IF YOU WANT TO.

KEEP GOING AND IT WILL EVEN BE POSSIBLE TO SCALE 'PANIC PEAK' WITHOUT FEAR.

THEY ARE ALL FEELINGS, CONSTRUCTED INSIDE YOU.

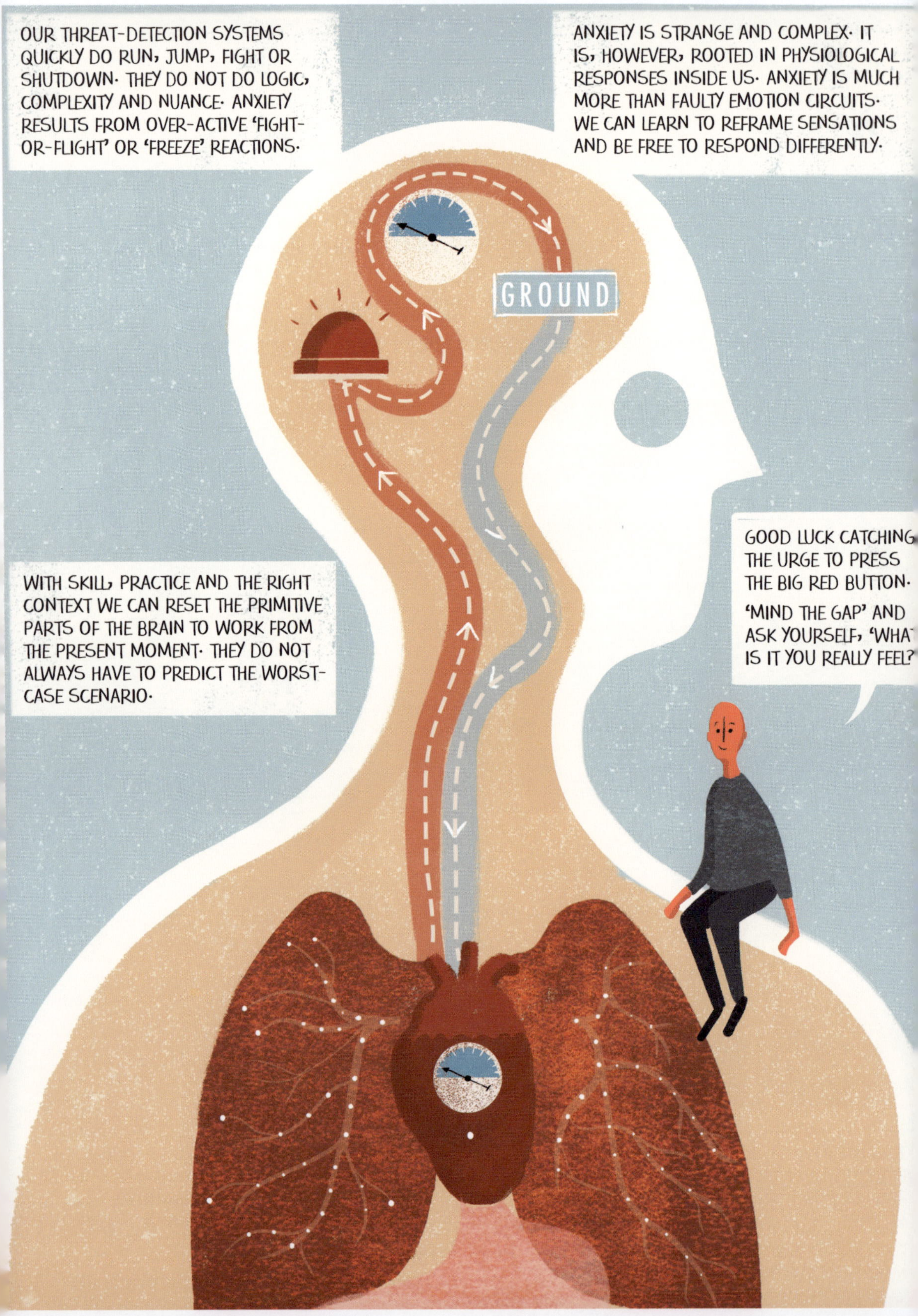

OUR THREAT-DETECTION SYSTEMS QUICKLY DO RUN, JUMP, FIGHT OR SHUTDOWN. THEY DO NOT DO LOGIC, COMPLEXITY AND NUANCE. ANXIETY RESULTS FROM OVER-ACTIVE 'FIGHT-OR-FLIGHT' OR 'FREEZE' REACTIONS.
ANXIETY IS STRANGE AND COMPLEX. IT IS, HOWEVER, ROOTED IN PHYSIOLOGICAL RESPONSES INSIDE US. ANXIETY IS MUCH MORE THAN FAULTY EMOTION CIRCUITS. WE CAN LEARN TO REFRAME SENSATIONS AND BE FREE TO RESPOND DIFFERENTLY.
GROUND
WITH SKILL, PRACTICE AND THE RIGHT CONTEXT WE CAN RESET THE PRIMITIVE PARTS OF THE BRAIN TO WORK FROM THE PRESENT MOMENT. THEY DO NOT ALWAYS HAVE TO PREDICT THE WORST-CASE SCENARIO.
GOOD LUCK CATCHING THE URGE TO PRESS THE BIG RED BUTTON. 'MIND THE GAP' AND ASK YOURSELF, 'WHAT IS IT YOU REALLY FEEL?'